Teaching Children Poetry

Photos and Poems by
Dwayne and Beth Cole

Teaching Children Poetry
ISBN: Softcover 979-8-89532-014-3
Copyright © 2023 by Charles Davidson

Parson's Porch Books is an imprint of Parson's Porch & Company (PP&C) in Cleveland, Tennessee. PP&C is a self-funded charity which earns money by publishing books of noted authors, representing all genres. Its face and voice is **David Russell Tullock** (dtullock@parsonsporch.com).

Parson's Porch & Company *turns books into bread & milk* by sharing its profits with the poor.

www.parsonsporch.com

Contents

Preface

The cover photo was taken at Potter Marsh, a nature preserve in Anchorage, Alaska. The swans migrate here from ice-free coastal and inland waterways to nest and raise their young. It shows a family of trumpeter swans, the world's largest member of water fowls. They weigh between 21 to 30 pounds. Some males weigh as much as 35 pounds. Like all swans, the male and female have identical all white plumage. They have a horn like call.

Both parents care for the young, usually keeping them in close range and sometimes lined up as in this picture.

Potter Marsh has a long wooden walkway with viewing areas that have large viewing scopes and sitting benches at several points. In the most bear and moose prone areas along the salmon streams, the board walk is elevated to protect visitors. It is a salmon sanctuary, and the abundance of salmon attracts black and brown bears.

This nature photo of a swan family with strong nurturing overtones seemed to be a good photo for this book cover, *Teaching Children Poetry*.

Introduction

When words become unclear, I shall focus with
photographs. —Ansel Adams

Children enjoy seeing pictures more than seeing words on
the page. In fact, this seems to be true of all ages.

Children also seem to feel an affinity with nature. From
personal experience, Beth and I found this to be true of our
childhood. I grew up on a farm. I spent a lot of time playing in
the woods and swinging from young hickory trees. I also
enjoyed playing at the mill rocks on Little Creek. I fished for
blue trout with red eyes and white suckers. Beth grew up in a
small town in West Tennessee, surrounded by a lot of farm
land.

We both experienced a love of nature with our children and
grandchildren. They enjoy our walks in nature observing its
beauty and wonder. This book is intended as an aid in

teaching children poetry. Every day children are learning new words.

What better time could there be to teach poetry. Parents and grandparents find this process of teaching poetry to children enjoyable also.

Beth and I enjoy poetry and wanted to share verses with our children and grandchildren, as a way to nurture openness with the beauty and wonder of nature. The three simple lines of the small haiku, have traditionally been seen as a good place to start teaching children a love of poetry.

Haiku uses inspiring nature scenes that enrich the lives of teacher and student. Our grandchildren's artwork and poems helped us re-discover a child's wonder

in our lives. Seeing the sparkle in their eyes helped us to see with the eyes of a child. The tears of joy washed away some of life's travel stains that cloud our vision.

The wonder of a child blossomed anew in us, becoming fertile ground for tender teachings.

I grew up in a farmhouse that was built from timber grown on the farm. When we used a tree, we planted or cultivated another, linking me to the magic of trees.

My childhood bedroom shared with 6 brothers was a porch closed in for sleeping, and at times you could count stars through the roof and exposed rafters. My 6 sisters had a nice bedroom they shared.

Mindful of that farmhouse, I wrote this haiku—

always very welcome
snowflakes falling on bed quilts
little boys' delight

Some Guidelines for Teaching Children Poetry

In teaching poetry to our grandchildren, we read poetry to them. Then as they thought of writing their own poems, we asked these questions to stimulate their poetic thoughts.

1. What is your poem going to be about?

2. Choose a subject from nature.

3. What nature images can you use to portray your subject.

4. Introduce the subject you have chosen in the first part of your poem.

5. Develop the theme or subject you have chosen.

6. In both haiku and sijo, bring the subject to a close with a twist in the third line of your haiku; and the last line in your sijo. The goal is to bring the subject to a close with a feeling of excitement. In haiku this is often an aha moment.

7. See my books listed in the chapters on different kinds of poetry for more guidelines.

Questions to ask children
while looking at pictures in this book

1.   What do you see in this photo?

2.   What is it speaking to you?

3.   What do you hear?

4.   Is there a bird language?

5.   Words express feelings. What do you feel?

6.   How can this help you be more sensitive to others?

7.   Can you write down what you see, hear, and feel?

Use the blank space below and the pages at the end of the book for you to write down your thoughts and shape them into poems.

I bring a flower
The sweetest I could find
Blossom kisses

(The snowshoe hare photo and poem are taken from my Haiku book shown here. See this book for other haiku poems.)

Haiku began in thirteenth-century Japan as the opening phrase of renga, a long poem. The short haiku broke away from renga in the sixteenth century. Haiku, using provocative, colorful images, focuses on a brief moment in time when we slow down and see nature scenes like an alpenglow sunrise or sunset transforming the whole sky.

Haiku has a deep appreciation of nature. Alaskans are closely related to luminous sparkling mountains, streams, and wildlife. Thus, haiku is especially suited to speak of the heartbeat of Alaska.

Haiku often ends with a surprising sense of enlightenment. It is in this aha moment, in empathy, that the songbird sings our heart awake, revealing truths from unknown realms. We see with new eyes and hear with new ears, moving into new adventures. We may not know where we are going, but we feel a new way has been opened. Kindness is in that Way.

The format of haiku is three lines, with the first and third lines each having 5 syllables, and the second line having 7 syllables. However, the emphasis is on three lines with an economy of words, not a total of 17 syllables. The syllable count may vary in each line—brevity that avoids overuse of metaphors and simile is key. Sensory experience is the goal.

Beth and I use Alaska nature photographs I have taken as inspiration for our haiku. Poetry inspired by art has been described as ekphrastic—meaning, to draw descriptive images out of the art.

The haiku and the photograph share the same space and often compliment each other. but not to explain one another. In some instances, the haiku and the photograph have little to do with one another. Each can stand alone.
Otherwise it would mean that one has been added because

the other is not complete or adequate to stand alone.

At the heart of nature haiku is a deep feeling of beauty. The wish to live and experience this beauty and wonder is visible in all living entities. In sharing this beauty,
we experience enlivenment—The deep meaning of life. Nature throbs with the desire to live. Haiku captures this beauty and sense of adventurous enlightenment, luring us toward more meaningful lives.

The following examples of haiku were written after viewing and photographing the family of swans at Potter Marsh.

Swan mates heart kissing

Trumpet and Reflect Good News
Love is Eternal

Trumpet the good news
Swan mates heart kissing
Love is so sweet

Trumpet the good news
Swan mates heart kissing
Valentines forever

Float on cool water
Be graceful trumpeter swans
Bob along with me.

Dip in the cool pond
Nestled in musical reeds
Sleep the night away.

Float by you forever
My graceful trumpeter swan
Nestled in our love

After haiku, sijo is a logical next step in teaching children poetry. Sijo is a Korean style of lyrical poetry originally called "short song." Sijo resembles Japanese haiku in having a foundation in nature, but neither sijo nor haiku are limited to nature as subject. Haiku is a short poem with three lines. The first and third lines have 5 syllables each, the second line has 7 syllables. The syllable count may vary slightly. The emphasis is on an economy of words.

Sijo has three lines with 14-16 syllables in each line, for a total of 44-46 syllables. The count may vary slightly as in haiku. In sijo, there is a pause in the middle of each line, so in English they are often printed in six lines instead of three, as can be seen below.

My Alaska Friends

We have many Alaska friends—
mountains, glaciers, waterfalls.

Moose, bears, eagles, and swans—
All re-wilding our lives with wonder.

Born from the wild things of nature—
Nurtured as one in heart and soul.

Safe in Ark

In the old farm beaver pond,
the guard slaps a warning sign.

The young dive into hut safely,
snug and secure from all harm.

Evolution's ark formation—
Home is a safe place to be.

(I grew up watching beavers build their hut in our farm pond.)

Swan Sijo

Two swans sail from azure sky,
 land barely leaving a ripple.

Float like a child's toy sail boats,
full of spices from foreign shores.

Child stands in awe seeing,
Santa delivering toys.

(Swan sijo taken from my book,
Heart Sijo: Alaska Inspired Photos and Poems).

Photos taken from our deck in Anchorage, Alaska

Black bear cubs of Alaska
love to climb elderberry bushes.

Mother Nature's tongue licking gifts,
dripping with sweetness on the tongue.

Mother stands on ground protecting.
Mothers everywhere are awesome.

(Taken from my Heart Sijo book)

Why Should We Teach Children Haiku and Sijo Poetry?

When teaching poetry from other cultures, you'll come across cultural ideas and idioms. Every language has idioms that come in all shapes and sizes. Korean culture is influenced by Confucian values—respect for family, elders, and authority.

Learning Japanese haiku and Korean sijo is a wonderful experience. You get a window into the history and wisdom of their language. In our culturally diverse world this can be a healthy healing experience.

An Asian proverb states: "It is better to see something once than to hear about it a thousand times." My hope for you is that these haiku, sijo, and other forms of poetry
will enable you to see life more clearly.

Chapter Three - Teaching Children Haibun

Haibun is a poem that starts with prose and ends with a haiku. The prose is often autobiographical. My book, *The Bible: A Poetic Journey* is filled with haibuns.

The Bible: A Poetic Journey, begins with this haibun on Genesis—

Genesis is the first book of the Bible. The Bible is the most popular book ever written. As of September 2022 all of the Bible has been translated into 724 languages, the New Testament has been translated into an additional 1,617 languages. *There are currently over 2,877 versions of the Bible in over 1,918 languages available digitally.*

The word, Genesis, originates from a Greek word that means beginning. The first part of the Book of Genesis
is about the beginning of all things, with special emphasis on the beginning of the people of Israel. Someone asked a Jewish Rabbi why God favored Israel. He responded; God calls all people. Israel heard and responded to the call that lures everyone toward beauty and love. The writers of Genesis were guided by this principle—

Out of darkness and chaos,
the world moves toward
light and goodness.

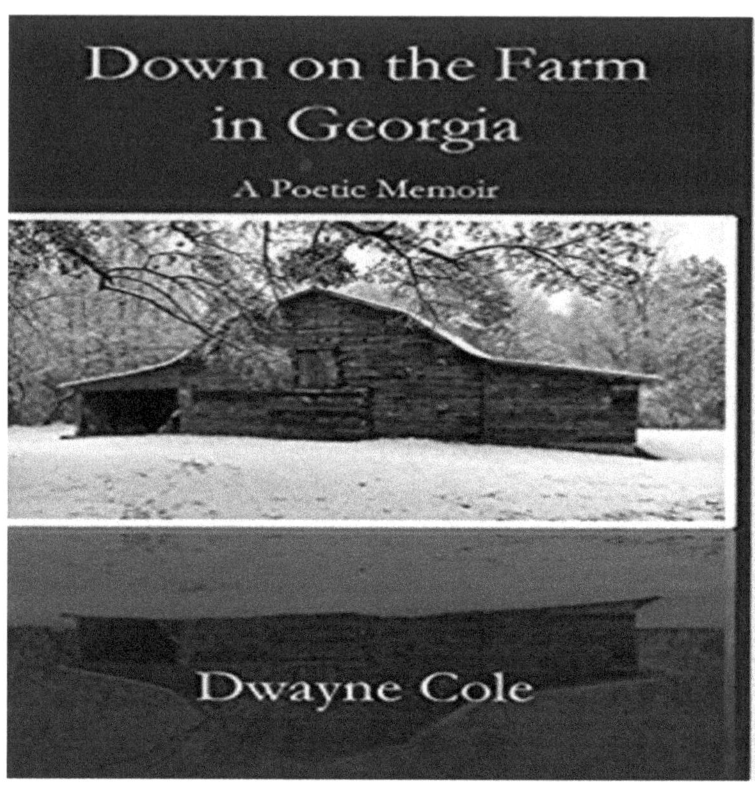

Farm House Haibun

I grew up in a farmhouse that was built from timber grown on the farm. When we used a tree, we planted or cultivated another, linking me to the magic of trees. My childhood bedroom shared with 6 brothers was a porch closed in for sleeping, and at times you could count stars through the roof and exposed rafters. My 6 sisters had a nice bedroom they shared. Our dear mother warmed old cast irons by the fireplace, wrapped them in a blanket, and placed them in our bed. to keep our feet warm.

Always very welcome
Snowflakes falling on bed quilts
Little boys' delight

A Moose Haibun

One spring day we were walking on the gravel road in Anchorage that leads to our daughter's house. We saw a young moose calf trying to cross the road. It would get half way and stop. Then turn back. His mother came part way back and stopped. The young moose joined its mother and they crossed together into a dandelion field. Then looking back at me, the mother seemed to say—

To get to Precious
You will have to come through me
Mothers are awesome

American Robins: Spring Is Here

Photos and Poems
by
Dwayne Cole

A limerick is a five-line poem that consists of a single stanza. Line one, traditionally starts with the phrase, "Once there was." The first, second and fifth lines end in a rhyme. The third and fourth lines are shorter and end in a rhyme. The subject is a short tale or description. Most limericks are funny.

Robin Limerick

This is a favorite limerick that I wrote for my book, *American Robins: Spring Is Here. This book with many different kinds of poems was written primarily for children ages 9-13.*

Once two robins came to our yard to play.

They announced, "Spring is on the way."

Grandchildren danced with joy.

They were like a windup toy.

Oh what a happy delightful day!

Birthday Limericks

(The first limerick below was written by my wife, Beth, for my birthday celebration. The second one by our grandchildren.)

A boy had a great birthday treat.
He could walk around on bare feet.
April 20 the day.
He"d run, skip, and play.
Birthday bard feet, what a treat!

We know of a grandpa we love
He likes to draw birds like a dove
He also writes verses
Without any curses
His poems come from above

Lynx Limerick

Once there was a beautiful lynx
Descendant of the mythical Sphinx
Golden eyes a prize
Ears of a large size
Oh the mystery of the lynx

White Peacock Butterfly photo
taken by my friend, George W. Reed

Butterfly Limerick

Once a white peacock butterfly.
Flapped its wings on the first try.
Basking in the sun.
Adds meaning to fun.
Beautiful art causes you to cry.

Chapter Five - Teaching Children Sonnets

**Black-Capped Chickadees:
Messengers of Hope**

**Photos and Poems
by
Dwayne Cole**

A Sonnet is a poem with fourteen lines that uses any of a number of formal rhyme schemes. In English a sonnet typically has ten syllables per line. However all definitions of poetry must be taken with a grain of salt. Historically, the poet has been granted freedom to alter syllable count, rhyme, and rhythm.

Chickadee Sonnet

Black-capped chickadees are such fun
Intent on stashing winter seeds
Feathers of hope, illumined by the sun.
Snowfall has just begun indeed.

Gather as many as you wish.
Devour to meet your needs.
High on my list is filling your dish
with sunflower heart seeds.

I'll never forget the wondrous feeling
the first time you landed in my hand.
Your bird language sent my heart reeling.

As long as you keep lighting in my hand,
I will write poems of love and kindness.
Your love is as true as a wedding band.

(This sonnet was taken from my poetry book,
Black-Capped Chickadees: Messengers of Hope).

Spring Robin Sonnet

Spring jonquils and American robins,

add in the mix, a silver birch tree.

Grandchildren a Bob Bob Bobbing.

Summer vacation, and all are so free.

Robins and jonquils and our true love,

live on in our memory and never die.

Our love is sealed by angels from above.

Spring robins do not tell us a lie.

Nature's values are truth, beauty, and love.

Values of society since Plato in ancient Greece.

At Jesus' baptism, the Spirit came as a dove.

We feel love in Jesus' tender teachings,

in Spring jonquils and American robins—

In grandchildren a Bob Bob Bobbing.

Love Sonnet

Trumpeter swan mates are heart kissing.
Trumpet the joyful good news far and wide.
Come and see what love you are missing.
In this family experience you can abide.

Trumpeter swan mates whispering secrets.
All nature is hopping and skipping along.
Blue skies are spreading picnic banquets.
Come experience love and add your song.

Swan mates heart kissing and caressing.
Trumpet the good news for all children.
Family love is truly refreshing.
.
Trumpet the good news far and wide.
Swan mates heart kissing with great pride.
Valentines are in love forever.

Chapter Six - Teaching Children Tanka

A tanka poem is a haiku with two additional lines of seven syllables each. Syllable count may vary slightly. Tanka uses vivid nature images. I wrote the three tanka below after photographing the swan family.

Float by you forever
My graceful trumpeter swan
Nestled in our love
Will build our nest together
Trumpeting a happy song

Float on cool water
Be graceful trumpeter swans
Bob along with you
Cygnets riding on our back
Nestled safely under wings

Dip in the cool pond
Nestled in musical reeds
Sleep the night away.
With cygnets bouncing on back
All whistling a happy tune

The world evolved
one flower at a time
Bees singing praise
Wherever there are flowers
There's hope of new beginnings

An acrostic is a poem in which the first letter in each line forms a word or phrase.

Steller's Jay Blue Sway

Photos and Poems
by
Dwayne Cole

I wrote this acrostic for my *Steller's Jay Blue Sway book*

Steller's Jay Acrostic

S cintillating beauty

T reasure of evolution

E nvy of Steller

L ovely blue skies

L oved by all

E very day wonder

R ise up and sing

S martest of birds

J oy of all bird watchers

A nthems of praise are due

Y ours truly, with love

Trumpeter Swan Acrostic

T wo mating swans

R raising cygnets

U under protective wings

M others are awesome

P apa keeps them in tow

E everyone important

T ender loving care

E expect the best

R each for stars

S now white feathers

W elcome to our shores

A ll have value

N ature is nurturing

(This acrostic welcomes all migrating birds, water fowl, and immigrants to our shores, while teaching family values and importance of saving our environment for future generations).

Pine Grosbeak Acrostic

P—Pretty as Christmas ornaments

I—Inspires awe and wonder

N—Nourishes love for all things

E—Evolution wonder

G— Gives more than is given

R—Resides in pine/spruce forest

O—Often feed in flocks when not mating

S—Sing beautiful songs

B—Beauty is own reason for being

E—Eats seeds, berries, insects

A—A welcome sight to birdwatchers

K—Kindness grows in reciprocal giving

Chapter Eight - Teaching Children Quatrain

Happy little redpolls swirling around seed dish.
Independent as stars shining in the Milky Way.
Gabriel's wings spread over our lives is my wish.
Tipping their red cap to kindness wins the day.

Quatrain is a complete poem of four lines, coming from many ancient cultures. They have many rhyme schemes. This one is ABAB— First and third lines end in a rhyme, and second and fourth end in a rhyme.

Copper River, home of Alaska's Best Salmon
42

Salmon Quatrain

In the long horizons salon eyes
I see glacier melt streams
Deep blue ocean dreams
Bluebird egg skies

Salmon roe hatching
Fingerlings navigating lakes
Flowing with rivers to oceans
Growing strong

Returning to streams
where they were spawned
Cycle begins anew
Nurturing mystery

I see in the salmon's eyes
Bluebird skies
Navigating river streams
Long horizon dreams

Viewing this picture, as well as the ones of moose and bear, remind me that we need to teach children how to be safe around wild animals. This photo was taken with a telescopic lens.

Magical Lynx Quatrain

To a child's imagination so keen
it was not merciless and mean.
It was just a kitty cat—
Magic pulled out of a hat.

Today a beautiful lynx,
descendant of the mythical Sphinx
came to visit, for free.
Sat regally under a tree.

Arctic Tern Quatrain

As the tern trims its sails
To make it through the gales
I faithfully banish fear
To make it through the year

(As I saw the arctic tern soaring, I asked, how do these champion migrators manage to travel 47,000 miles each year from the Arctic to the Antarctic. Tossed about with icy gales and shaken by storm currents. They just appear as if conjured by Mother Nature's magic wand.)

Chapter Nine-Teaching Children Free-Style Poetry

Swan Family

Two swans sail down
Out of azure skies

Land on water
Barely leaving a ripple

Float across pond
A child's toy sail boats

Filled with spices
Born from foreign shores

Many other treasures
Only the child knows

Imaginary gifts so free
Fill the child with glee

Swans open their wings
Catch the updraft of gentle breeze

Child stands in awe
Seeing Santa delivering toys

He waves
Swans rise higher and higher

Wings will soon touch another shore
Another child to please

Part II

Gifts from heaven come
In tremors of sunlight

Tender and luminous
Gifts we cannot see

Soft as feathers light
Sparkling on calm waters

Bathed in light
Washed and transformed

Heaven's glory
Comes down

Light we cannot see
But eternally do

Alleluia!
Alleluia!

Part III

Sitting quietly
Pondering

How the universe moves
Toward the production of beauty

Eyes fall on
Newspaper headlines

COVID-19 cases rise

Protesters rally
Calling for end to racism

Fall on knees
Prayerfully asking

What have we done
To contribute beauty

Nurturing
The precious gift of life

What I hope
And trust today—

The dazzling light we cannot see
Yet eternally do

Is far greater
Than despair and death

Heals
Transforms

Walk in the light!

Let it shine!
Let it shine!

Chapter Ten - Teaching Children Couplets

A couplet is poetry that has one thought in two lines. The lines can be rhymed, but they don't have to rhyme.
Couplets can be used to form longer poems. The previous long poem with three parts is composed mainly with couplets. Below are a couple examples of couplets.

Northern Lights, burning bright,
shining in the night.

On wings of hope
two swans land in the lake.

Even shorter than couplets are single line poems.
The Pulitzer Prize winning poet, Mary Oliver, used these often and called them sand dabs. An example from Mary is "Are morning kisses the sweetest?" For children, you might say, "Are Mother's morning kisses the sweetest?"

.

Can you write a few couplets and one-line poems below?

Conclusion - Value of Teaching Children Poetry

The central purpose of teaching poetry to children is to become one with the beauty and wonder of nature. In the photos of the swan family, I see stars twinkling—I see a spinning universe. In that moment, I am participating in the beauty of life. I experience the gift of wonder.

> We contemplate in nature in order
> to understand our existence in the natural world. We become a part of what we think about. In these moments we are actively becoming a part of nature.
>
> This encounter with nature is for awakening a new self-understanding. Swans, as all water fowls and birds, become symbolic of release from bondage. Viewing them we become kin, friends, giving us wings. We see new possibilities of soaring with them in blue skies.
>
> Heaven shines on us
> Healing our broken spirit
> Angels singing praise

The Purpose of this Book

In Conclusion, lets pause for a moment and reflect on how this book came to be—

My wife, Beth, and I retired to Alaska in 2011, to become caregivers of grandchildren, as our daughter and son-in-law started their medical practices.

In that move, I became a photographer/poet. All the natural beauty and wonder of Alaska spoke to me saying, "Take my picture. Write a poem about me."

Alaska, the last wild frontier, is so beautiful, so very beautiful! I daily take pictures of Alpenglow sunrises and sunsets, and occasionally the Aurora Borealis. Glaciers, waterfalls, cascading streams, rivers and lakes are abundant in Alaska.

Moose and bears are an almost daily presence. Alaska has one moose for every four citizens, and one bear for every five. Both moose and bears have walked through automatic opening glass doors in seeking food.

Our poetry speaks of the beauty and wonder, magical music of the spheres, coming on wings of inspiration.

This book, *Teaching Children Poetry,* was *inspired by one of our favorite quotes from Einstein:*

"Look deep into nature, and then you will understand everything better."

In making this journey into nature—

No ticket is needed
Nature's not a place to just visit
It's home every day

Let's open our hearts
In compassion to each other
Let kindness blossom

In nature poetry
We see radiance of all things
An epiphany

Appendix: How To Use This Book

Many of the photos and poems in this book were shared with our grandchildren from the time they started to kindergarten in 2011, and until they finished high school. We wanted to create a love for nature poetry and the beauty of birds. If you wish to accomplish this wonder in your life and share it with others, the suggestions below will be helpful.

1. It is hard to look at the pictures and poems without feeling joy and happiness. Take time for this; and if children are involved, let them express their happiness. You might turn some of the photos into a game of I spy. Do you see what I see?

2. One of the purposes of this book is to teach kindness toward all living things, and especially toward all children. Ask how we can show kindness? (See my book, *Kindness Is Every Step).*

3. Use this book, *Teaching Children Poetry*, as inspiration for learning proper use of cameras and photo techniques.

4. If you are sharing the book with children or youth, you might want to teach color pencil drawing of birds and nature scenes. Our grandchildren loved this activity. As they get older you can move to watercolors and oil painting.

This is one of the early color pencil drawings I did with our grandchildren.

5. My wife, Beth, and I wanted to teach children to write nature poems. Many of the poems in this book are haiku. Haiku has been seen as a good way to start learning and teaching poetry. Sijo is the logical next step in this poetic adventure.

6. My books, *Heart Haiku: Alaska Inspired Photos and Poems;* and *Heart Sijo: Alaska Inspired Photos and Poems,* will be helpful in understanding and teaching these forms of poetry. These books can be purchased on line from Parson's Porch Books, Amazon, and Barnes & Noble.

7. Let your love of children guide you in finding other creative ways to use this book. Send me your ideas., please

Your Response

The following pages are left blank intentionally for you and your children to write a poem or two on each of the kinds of poems described in this book. Also, for you to record your response and your ideas for teaching children poetry. Please consider sending me your response for improving this book for future editing.

Ten Commandments of Children's Poetry to Help Shape Your Poems

1. Keep it simple

2. Lots of action

3. Has children as actors

4. Sees from a child's point of view

5. Shows hope and optimism

6. Uses fantasy

7. Uses humor

8. Tap into creativity

9. Help develop reading skills

10. Learn about other cultures

BOOKS BY DWAYNE COLE

(My wife, Beth, is a professional editor, and made major contributions to the 35 books I have published. I list my books here as aids in teaching nature poetry. Many of the poems in these books were first used with our children and grandchildren to help them grow along with the beauty and wonder of nature.)

A Center that Holds: Adventures in Kindness

Alpenglow Miracles: Fire Dance of Wonder

Alzheimer's: A Minister's Guide

American Robins: Spring Is Here

A Prayer of Blessing: As You Go Remember This

A Relational Hermeneutic of Kindness

A Relational Trinity of Kindness

BEARS AND MOOSE OF ALASKA: Nature Poetry

Black-Capped Chickadees: Messengers of Good News

Clouds of Inspiration

Down on the Farm in Georgia: A Poetic Memoir

Dragonfly Magic

Gentle Galilean Glories: The Tender Teachings of Jesus

God and Evil: An Ode to Kindness

Heart Haiku: Alaska Inspired Photos and Poems

Heart Sijo: Alaska Inspired Photos and Poems

How to Teach Children Poetry

Jesus: Poet of the World

Jesus' Transforming Beatitudes: Selected Sermons from Year A

Jesus' Transforming Love: Selected Sermons from Year B

Jesus' Transforming Gentle Teachings: Selected Sermons from Year C

Kindness Is Every Step

Lone Leaf Dancing

Poems Inspired by Process Philosophy

Poet of the Universe: A Vision of Beauty and Goodness.

Rainbows of Hope

Snowshoe Hare Beauty

Steller's Jay Blue Sway

The Apostles' Creed: A Living Creed for the Living Church.

The Bible: A Poetic Journey